REQUIEM
with AN
AMULET
in ITS
BEAK

REQUIEM
with AN
AMULET
in ITS
BEAK

poems

ELIZABETH KNAPP

2019 Jean Feldman Poetry Prize Winner

Washington Writers' Publishing House
Washington, D.C.

COVER ART by Steven Spazuk
COVER DESIGN by Meg Reid
BOOK DESIGN by Barbara Shaw

Library of Congress Cataloging-in-Publication Data
Names: Knapp, Elizabeth, author.
Title: Requiem with an amulet in its beak : poems / Elizabeth Knapp.
Description: First edition. | Washington, D.C. : Washington Writers'
   Publishing House, [2019]
Identifiers: LCCN 2019022668 | ISBN 9781941551202 (paperback)
Classification: LCC PS3611.N35 A6 2019 | DDC 811/.6—dc23
LC record available at https://lccn.loc.gov/2019022668

Printed in the United States of America

WASHINGTON WRITERS' PUBLISHING HOUSE
P. O. Box 15271
Washington, D.C. 20003

for Cody Dylan Todd (1978 – 2016)

CONTENTS

∞

∞

But listen, I am warning you
I'm living for the very last time.

— Anna Akhmatova

This life & no other.

— Larry Levis

∞

"YOUR LIFE IS MEANINGLESS"

I cannot tell you where they came from.
It seemed they appeared from the sky,
rounding the corner in their silver Camry
like a spaceship from another galaxy.
College kids, or so I thought, drunk
as shit but still clean cut, the type
you'd expect to play varsity lacrosse
and to love their mothers a bit
too much, the kind who'll go on
to become management executives
or investment analysts with two houses
and ex-wives in three separate cities.
So when one of them leaned
out of the passenger side window
and yelled those words to no one
ahead of or behind me on the street,
I chuckled to myself but never stopped,
safe in my womb of obliviousness,
until I realized he was talking to *me*.
Something miraculous happened
at that moment, something I cannot
begin to describe, but as I continued
on, straight from my appointment
with the OB/GYN, where I saw him
swimming on a flat, black screen,
a shadow creature just barely visible,
a Rorschach test to anyone but me,
never in my life had my life held
more meaning, never had I felt more
achingly alive, the insight carrying me,
until together we began to float,
soon-to-be mother and not-yet child,
along the empty, dead-end street.

CAPITAL I

Some days I don't know myself
from you, or you from your reflection,
which in truth is neither his, nor mine,

nor even your own, but something as yet
undefined, unfixed, like the stars peeling
from the Milky Way on the ceiling,

or the donut hole closing softly in your head.
Some days I don't know myself from me,
can't shake the stubborn feeling

I've been abducted by aliens
and brainwashed into believing
that there is no actual *self* to protect,

only a sack of sleepless nerves
which would, no doubt, spill everything
under torture. So when all through that first

bewildering summer, as we watched
vintage *Sesame Street* over and over—
"Capital I," and "lowercase n,"

the melancholic strains of 70s folk guitar—
I felt the cleaving of new selfhood begin,
the labor pains of the I I was birthing,

even as you became the you you are,
the you you're still becoming.
Darling, there is no I high in the sky

for you to polish up and keep.
The world will steal you soon enough.
The I will make you weep.

MY PAST LIFE AS A SONGBIRD

In this life, I should have been most happy. Nary a care in the world, save for the constant pressure of having to marry the need for a mate with a tune. I sang like the last living creature on earth, burning out my syrinx until the air vibrated like the strings of some heavenly harp, calling me back to the fold, though deep down I knew it was all just wishful thinking. What did I have to live for? A nest full of hatchlings and a drowned-out song? At least I wasn't lying.

FIFTH YEAR: WOOD

Not Blake's bitter "Poison Tree" or the bedpost
carved from olive by Odysseus's hand,
but a potted Chinese bonsai, its newborn leaves
an incandescent green, its wired trunk knotted
and scarred. You stare at the empty box at your feet.
Is five years long enough to know exactly
what you're thinking? Something else to keep
alive in this house of needful things, one more
ward under our charge (what do we know
of husbandry?), cutting back its wayward roots
and every year replanting. So much upkeep
required. Better to give you a toothpick, a match-
stick, a fine chopping block. Sixth year's gift:
an iron poker. Save this one for kindling.

SONG WHILE THE CHILDREN ARE NAPPING

You who said you would never write
a domestic poem in your life,
praise this moment of silence,
the house a still life of chaos:
the overturned sippy cup,
the macaroni ground into the carpet
from lunch, the plastic stegosaurus
you nearly killed yourself on, stumbling
into the kitchen this morning.
Praise this stolen moment,
its second chances, the glimpse
of what you might accomplish
if you would just sit down and write,
no matter how banal or uninspiring
your immediate surroundings.
Praise the uninspiring most of all.

PALOMAS, CIUDAD DE MÉXICO

Because devotion. Because ether. Because the saint holds a paintbrush, his sorrow. Because the grass may grow sharply, its knives. Because wonder. Because somehow a dove has nailed itself to the shadow of a tree. Because at some point in this holy story, a wrought iron door is opening. Because we could not speak for ourselves, we let the molecules do the talking. Because the power lines, the city. Because the city, the fires. Because each square of hope turned out to be hopeless, we let our eyes roam as they pleased. Because the painter's gaze, no exit. Because illegible the text of the dove's scarred wings.

SELF-PORTRAIT AS KURT COBAIN
WRESTLING WITH THE ANGEL

Here, the biblical allusion is a metaphor for the speaker's internal
struggles, and since Cobain is the persona, one can infer that the
speaker may be alluding to her own struggles with depression and/or
addiction. While this may be partly true, the beauty of metaphor is
its ability to retain multiple meanings simultaneously, like the angel
which in reality is no angel but a dark stich inside the speaker who
for years took it to be a birthmark or a fatal flaw or the mark of Cain.
So too Cobain: lake of fire in the pit of the stomach. He who wrestles
with God wrestles with himself. The beauty of metaphor is that the
angel can be just an angel if you let it.

THE YOUNG VIRGIN

after the painting by Francisco de Zurbarán

To pray as she does
   beyond belief into the palm
     of belief itself stillness

     like a held breath or a curtain
   drawn for a moment we are
witness to her waiting her

womb an empty vivarium
   around her head cherubs-
     to-be halo around her

     hymnody of needle
   and thread the raiment
of her youth she will wait

until the lilies in the urn begin
   to brown and curl and the book
     opens to a page from which

     the angel enters we will
   watch as she receives him
and draws inside her Lord

FAITH

The way George Michael sang it,
even I, an apostate, believed.
With every sway of his denimed hips,
steel-toed boots tapping away
against the shrine of the jukebox,
gold cross earring glittering against
the ragged shadow of his jaw,
I fell further into faith. If you
were a teenaged girl growing up
in the 80s, you fell too, I guarantee it.
In high school, I had a friend
who seduced our middle-aged
chemistry teacher to the tune
of "Father Figure" in his backyard
one summer afternoon. I remember
her telling me how his fingers felt
as he rubbed sunscreen over her half-
naked body, lingering just there
at the edge of her bikini, before falling
headlong into faith himself. Later,
after he'd been fired, she played
"One More Try" over and over,
as if the past were a blackboard
she could erase. It's almost
faded now, a track on the mix-
tape of someone else's youth. Still,
sometimes when the body hears
the memory of that music, it's holy.

THRENODY WITH A WHITE FORD BRONCO INSIDE IT

That was the night I lost my virginity
   to a boy who wore a trench coat
      and played Dungeons & Dragons,

while my friend's ex-Navy Seal dad
   slept soundly in the room below.
      The boy had crawled through a window.

He tried to kill himself, once.
   That night the Rockets played
      the Knicks in the NBA Finals,

Hakeem the Dream leaping
   across the court like a gazelle,
      then falling to his knees in prayer,

Clyde the Glide moving in
   for the rebound, then the whisper
      of a swoosh. My friend and I ate cheese

quesadillas with Newman's Own
   salsa as we watched. I can tell you
      the exact moment America died,

but the truth is it had died
   many times, we'd just never bothered
      to look. O, America, you left

whatever happiness you believed
   was your birthright in the glove
      compartment of an SUV driven

by a sociopath with a gun to his head
    on an empty freeway in a city
        of bystanders, the black wings

of helicopters spurring him on.
    The night it happened, the ghost
        of Kurt Cobain howled from the radio,

as moonlight seeped into the eyelet
    bedspread. Like a dog, you walked
        through your own master's blood.

KOKO THE GORILLA IS DEAD

I wanted to write an elegy for the gorilla
    who famously learned sign language

from a researcher who believed that apes
    had something to teach us about being

human, a lesson on empathy and living
    in the moment, but that was the summer

I almost gave up being human myself,
    time a primordial soup I wanted to drown in,

nothing but the flat raft of breath holding
    me up. That summer, migrant children cried

at the barbed wire border, while in a hotel
    near Strasbourg, everyone's favorite drifter

hanged himself with his belt. That summer
    America was at war with itself, careening

into itself like a Patriot missile to the tune
    of "Won't You Be My Neighbor," a speck

of wood smoldering in its eye. That was
    the summer I wanted to die, watching

video clips of Koko tickling the bipolar
    comedian. Later, after she learned of his death,

she clutched his photo to her massive
    breast and made the sign for "Why?"

SELF-PORTRAIT AS KURT COBAIN'S CHILDHOOD WOUND

If I were Kurt's childhood wound, what would I look like? The speaker stares off into the middle distance and tries to imagine Aberdeen, mid-70s, a flaxen-haired kid who would become the next rock legend, and not the gaping hole of his left eye socket or the brain matter, scattered like jewels across the floor. (Bless thy sweet eyes, they bleed.) *The thing is, I think Kurt's fatal wound and his childhood wound were one and the same, just as the new generation carries the wounds of the old generation like prison tattoos to its grave.* The speaker isn't satisfied with this comparison, as "prison tattoos" does not convey the depth of Cobain's wounding, or the world's, or even her own. There is, however, the nice slant-rhyme of "same/grave," which is far less Whitmanian and far more genocidal than may at first seem. What grows there grows everywhere. The wound is a hole covered by weeds.

HUNTER'S MOON, GETTYSBURG

I could have believed anything
        that night, on that one-lane
                country road, the battlefield
        alive with shadows, outlines
                of worm fences where X

marks the spot, cupolas
        of blackened barns, and beyond,
                the far slope of Cemetery Hill,
        where ghost troops huddled
                under the broken moonlight,

and the wind made anguished
        sounds with its breath. Yes,
                it was still possible for the world
        to surprise me, or rather, it was
                still possible to surprise myself,

even there, waist-deep
        in the trenches, but crawling
                my way out, up along the ravaged
        hillside, to where, from a distance,
                the carnage looked gorgeous.

SIXTH YEAR: IRON

After a heated debate about the nature
of inspiration (poetry versus prose),
with you arguing that idea begets word,
and not vice versa, as I believe is the case

with verse (always the music first),
which was prompted by a discussion
of Dickinson's envelope poems,
and whether she wrote the poem

to fit the shape of the paper, or she shaped
the paper to fit the poem (both, I think),
I decided to try it your way: to hold
the idea of the poem in mind

before ever hearing its words,
to follow it like an iron horse
through the valley of imagination,
until it disappeared at a bend in the track

into a landscape I couldn't see.
Enter these cast iron bookends
(knights in shining armor just for Gus),
signposts to mark where one mile ends

and another begins in the uncharted road
of matrimony. Forgive me, love,
I was running out of time. I didn't know
what I would give until I wrote this.

MY PAST LIFE AS A DINOSAUR

for Gus

Naturally, I was an herbivore, one of the gentle giants with four or more hearts and a placid expression I carried even to the end. I spent most of my time grazing treetops—redwoods, pines, yews—anything I could reach, and I cared for my young the way any good sauropod would—by leaving them where they hatched and letting them fend for themselves. The gastroliths in my gizzard churned something fierce, but I didn't mind, because the air up there was so much cleaner. I breathed it in through the top of my head, and when the sky lit up like an electric fence, I didn't flinch, knowing I would come back one day as a superhero.

STARMAN TRACTATE: CHAMELEON, COMEDIAN, CORINTHIAN, AND CARICATURE

Somewhere, on an alternate plane under the earth's surface, someone is writing a series of David Bowie poems. This someone is in fact an alternate version of yourself, a shadow-ego, so to speak, and she has dark hair and eyes and can be heard late at night scratching her poems onto the linoleum of her kitchen floors, which are actually your ceilings, if you're sleeping upside down. Never mind that she only wears white or that she rarely showers. She could be the next Emily Dickinson, for all you know. You tolerate her, because it gives you solace knowing some simulacrum of yourself is also mourning his loss. And besides, on some level, you know her Bowie poems are better.

THE MARTIAN

My mind is all wheels.
      Four years ago this sol,

I became the only other
      I know. Take this selfie,

for example—how my one
      roving eye stares back

at itself with a look almost
      disquieting in its directness,

which is why I prefer
      to focus on the mission:

clouds of red silt and the ever-
      elusive presence of water,

alluvial fan like the lines
      of an open human palm.

Everywhere you go,
      there's nowhere to get to,

so I bumble on, a bee
      in a garden, sampling

each specimen, my
      aluminum members

all lit and engorged.
      Happy birthday to me,

I sing to the impact craters.
   Happy birthday to me,

I sing to Olympus Mons.

SELF-PORTRAIT AS THE LOVE CHILD
OF KURT COBAIN AND EMILY DICKINSON

From him, I inherited a translucency of eyes and complexion, which, in the arena of stardom, means I'm constantly haunted by the glare, his blue veins creeping up my arms like lichen. From her, my Puritan obsession with recycling and a closet full of housedresses. Naturally, I'm an introvert of the most introverted sort. I keep versions of myself under glass where I can occasionally do experiments on them, as the mood strikes. Unlike my parents, I didn't drop out of school, though they did engender in me a certain distrust of authority, a punk sensibility in some ways seasoned by their deaths. I won't say I miss them, though sometimes when the wind blows through me, I can almost hear them sing.

ELEGY WITH A CAMEO BY LINDA RONSTADT
for my father

You aren't dead, but something
in the honeyed scythe

of her voice smote me
there in the middle of Target,

left me weeping in the aisles,
mourning you, and by extension,

mourning myself, remembering
how you would lift each record

like a skiff and place it gently
on the table, adjusting

the needle's arm until the crackle
of music began. I loved the skips

the most, how you would grumble,
cursing, knocking on the shelf,

how a minute would repeat
in an endless motorcade of hours,

and this was called
childhood, as I understood it.

Neither of you was gone,
yet at that moment my own life

skipped, and for a moment
I heard its silence.

AFTER THE FLOOD

Something had changed in those who had
witnessed it, so that when they opened
their front doors, squinting into the light,
what had once been a concrete sprawl
appeared to them as the oceans of heaven,
crests glinting in the late afternoon sun,
as the hum of motorboats ruptured
the silence, goldbeaters on the water's skin.
No one remembered the days leading up
to it—how the birds grew strangely quiet,
how the horses crossed the sudden fields
as if spooked by their own shadow, how
everyone went on about their business
behind the wheel in the kingdom of God.

IS THAT A GUN IN YOUR POCKET

Because we could not look you in the eye,
we turned to social media. In your suburbs,
yard signs blossomed, dollars spent
and deposited themselves. Everywhere,
carnivals returned to fashion, particularly those
employing clowns. When I say *we*, I mean
the dark that seeds the fear of itself.
Summer evenings still featured sprinklers
and baseball for the sake of fans,
but everyone agreed the sun seemed shaky.
By *everyone*, I mean the collective dream
we restream each night. America,
in one tiny fist you held a bottle of pills
marked *Amnesia*; in the other, a concealed .45.

MINORITY REPORT

Imagine an alternate future
in which Tom Cruise

is elected president.
I'm not saying

it could really happen,
but imagine a future

in which the state
is one gigantic eyeball

that never blinks.
In this perversion

of Emersonian
Transcendentalism,

the group mind is such
that any deviation

is treated with the utmost
suspicion. Thus,

anyone who uses *thus*
in a poem will be summarily

executed. I'm not saying
it's going to happen,

but sooner or later,
somebody somewhere

is going to blow himself up.

FOURTH OF JULY

In America, we like our flags fried
and rolled in powdered sugar,
which is why fireworks always remind us
of bombs, the shock and awe
of a mighty nation. After the parade,
I feel an overwhelming urge
to take a hot shower, Americana
like grease over everything. If you asked
two of us the same question, you'd get
six different answers, depending
on which side of the news you're on.
On the outskirts of town, a band is playing
well into the night. Some of us are sleeping.
Some would kill us in our sleep.

BLACK FRIDAY

So that we can kill each other more efficiently,
doors will remain open into eternity. 50%
off all merchandise, including your sanity.
Items may be returned for a full refund
in hell. Passing by the display cases, my body
could be any body out for a stroll in the aisles
of America, where packs of app-crazed
Millennials swipe under the unblinking eye
of a drone. At the local Walmart, Camo Barbie
sits next to a box of shotgun shells, pink
AR-15 included. Because we can't get away
from ourselves fast enough, we let shiny
objects distract us, all that we see but dare not
touch inside the showrooms of our avarice.

MY BRAIN IS MAD FOR BAUDRILLARD

Today, I read of scientists' warnings
about the potential dangers of sex
robots and thought of you. Some blame
the rise of right-wing populism
on postmodern windbags like you, holed
up in your university office, giving head
to your shadow. But Jean, you were right—
we *are* living in the desert of the real,
where signs metastasize like cancer cells,
and who hasn't felt the Foucauldian
grip around her wrists, her ankles?
Even desire a simulacrum of itself.
I drowned in you as if in a frozen lake,
but either I or the lake was dreaming.

SELF-PORTRAIT AS CINDY SHERMAN'S INSTAGRAM ACCOUNT

And why not Sherman herself, you ask?
Because in this instance, the inclusion
of social media denotes a postmodern
approach to self-portraiture, a Baudrillardian
hall of mirrors in which the self is projected
against a million anonymous eyes, all hungry
for a taste of her. How will she deform
herself next? Will she sport a new prosthetic
chin, her hair stand on end, electrocuted?
A Dr. Frankenstein in the lab with herself.
A million followers, and not one will ever
know her—nipped, tucked, and bruised beyond
all recognition. *Das Umheimliche*: an unhomely
home. A rubber crotch on a mannequin.

SELF-PORTRAIT AS KURT COBAIN IN DRAG

In this self-portrait, Cobain is the personification of the speaker's rage. His dressing in drag represents the gender fluidity the speaker feels 90% of the time, although this may be the result of exposure to certain polyurethane products, particularly the foam in the sofas of a certain Swedish furniture manufacturer. Who wants to read a poem that explains itself? *I do, I do!*

So in this self-portrait, the speaker as Cobain in drag is drop-dead fucking gorgeous, with her sky-eyed junkie stare and her Christ bod fresh from the cross. As a woman, she can be a man becoming a woman becoming a poet becoming a god. She can feed on herself—a loaf of bread or a single glistening fish—her plate empty as the star she rode in on.

Finally, consider the relationship between Cobain's message and the speaker's own. Is this someone you'd want instructing your children, nihilism sprayed on the classroom walls and pronouns slipped on like condoms? Now diagram this sentence: I want to be raped by the world.

Misunderstood poet-god strung out in petticoats, isn't this what you asked for, a stage to playact your fantasies of grandeur and oblivion and an audience who's paid to care?

MY PAST LIFE AS A PURITAN

According to Wikipedia, I was possessed by the devil from late 1671 to early 1672, a 16-year-old servant in the house of a certain Samuel Willard, a prominent preacher in the town of Groton, Massachusetts, who recorded my possession using a methodical scientific approach highly unusual for the time. Willard, who became my "Gate Keeper," detailed every moment of my 10-week sojourn with Satan, and later became active in the Salem Witch Trials, which he argued should be conducted in a "fair and legal way." No one knows what happened to me after his journals end. (Some reports claim I turn up centuries later on a lark.)

SEVENTH YEAR: WOOL

I considered titling this "Love Poem
in Which I Pull the Wool over Your Eyes,"
but the truth is you knew exactly
what you were getting into, just as
we both know that marriage is anything
but a pair of wool socks stored away
for sub-freezing days when the world
is too callous to notice lovers warming
their lips in parks, or the transient
warming their souls by fires set
by arsonists' rage. No delusions
here, and anyway, you hate wool:
something else to make you itch
for the life you gave up for this bitch.

SELF-PORTRAIT AS KURT COBAIN'S MUSE

No, I'm not his ragdoll whore or the shade of a post-punk feminist icon.
I do not resemble a seahorse in the slightest, though I can paddle like
the dickens under water. I did not lure him like some pierced-tongue
Siren, nor did I ever turn him into a farm animal, though plenty of times
I thought about it. He came to me already broken, like a bird with one
clipped wing. *Here, let me clip the other.*

LAST TANGO IN PARIS

I walked all over the streets of Paris,
searching for the ghost of Marlon Brando.

I wandered the Jardin du Luxembourg,
the seedy bits of La Pigalle,
down to the Quai d'Orléans,

where I found him shagging
the shadow of his former self.

This was back in 1972,
when the talk was short
and the sex was long.

Whatever he said that night,
it was lost in the moonlight
and in the uncanny sound
of a man's mind cleaving.

He was so drunk
I had to carry him home.

POEM IN THE MANNER OF THE YEAR
IN WHICH I WAS BORN

Little poem, you are too young to remember
the smoking gun, the con man on TV
who looked like a supervillain, or the hominid
skeleton dug up in Africa and given the name
of your childhood dog. You never heard a word
about the IRA bombings, nor did *The Texas Chainsaw
Massacre* terrorize your sleep. Having no use
for money, you do not understand the concept
of stagflation, nor did you marvel at the satellite
images of Jupiter's Great Red Spot. How much
you have missed in the span of half a century!
I want to swaddle you in yesterday's headlines
and send you back down the river, no wiser
than the day you came blaring into the world.

EIGHTH YEAR: BRONZE

Baby, be my Babylonia.
I'll be Hammurabi
to your hanging gardens

and you can be my ziggurat.
I want to plow your lower
Euphrates. I want to smelt

you over an open fire
until we make a new alloy,
until your Aegean

laps at the shores
of my Knossos. Let's
pioneer the potter's wheel

and invent a cuneiform
only we can decipher.
Later, when they excavate

the carbonized imprint
of our embrace, they'll say
we were the first to prosper.

STARMAN TRACTATE: LET ALL THE CHILDREN BOOGIE

When I was a child, I sang like a child. I channeled my inner Ziggy and tattooed a lightning bolt on my left shoulder. When I became an adult, I put the ways of the Starman behind me. It is sad because the days are long and yet the years fly by. How was it only yesterday he was here and still already a ghost? Dapper as all get-out in that black fedora. Grinning like he knows something we don't.

SELF-PORTRAIT AS KURT COBAIN'S IMAGINARY FRIEND

In the end, I could not save him. For years, he carried me around in the cigar box where he kept his stash, like a side of himself he didn't want anyone to see. They blame me for all his wrongdoings—the bullying, the stealing, the cat he trapped up his parents' chimney—but the truth is, I set him free. Without me, he would have been just another junkie littering the streets. His last words were addressed to me: *Dear Boddah, I think I simply love people too much*. Dear Kurt, experienced simpleton, emasculated, infantile complainee, I was the I in your denial. I was the needle to your insatiable need.

LAMENT IN THE STYLE OF
MONICA LEWINSKY'S BLUE DRESS

Where do you suppose she keeps it?
Tucked away in the back of her closet
next to the unworn J.Crew wedding dress,
for those of us feeling sentimental,
or for the rest of us who don't give a fuck,
or at the very least who don't remember,
maybe she torched it, a bonfire fueled
by partisanship, as the twentieth century
smoldered. Either way, she owned it,
never sold the rights to the sex museum
on the Vegas Strip, or wrapped it up
in newsprint and left it on the steps
of Congress. No sense in crying
anymore. Even the hangers are lonely.

MEDITATION
after Baudelaire

Settle down now, sadness. It's time for bed.
You asked for evening. Well, here it is.
A fine mist covers the city like dread.
It may look peaceful, but trust me, it isn't.

People can be vile, especially large crowds
of people lashed by the bloody whip
of pleasure, reaping remorses like stones.
Come on, sadness, take my hand, let's

go. Watch the years die most unfashionably,
leaning too far over heaven's balcony,
wearing yesterday's wedding dress. Smiling,
regret really knows how to work a room.

The sun's half-asleep. It's nearly dead under
the vaulted arch of sky. Listen, my dear,
can you hear it? Night on tiptoe at the top
of the stairs, trailing a shroud behind it.

THE YEAR OF THE ECLIPSE

The moon was so quiet, we hardly
noticed the sun's absence. Gradually,
the land went dark, pasture by steaming
pasture. One could step outside
and everything would seem normal—
the hedged lawns, traffic lights
still blinking as they should under a sky
we never assumed to be permanent.
But one by one the candles burned out,
city grids flickered in the mist, until all
that was left of love was the idea of love
behind the curtain of sudden nightfall,
shadow draped over the earth as if over
a casket. Then the closing of the lid.

REQUIEM WITH AN AMULET IN ITS BEAK

At night, I leave all the lights on in my head.
This way, I know the dead can find me.

Sometimes they toss me their worldly trinkets:
the moon, wobbly as a child's loose tooth,
a tuning fork, a spear of lightning for my song.

Like a magpie, I collect them.
I line my own death-nest
with the baubles of the dead.

Nothing, not even death, can harm me.

THE CEMETERY IS FULL OF PEOPLE WHO
WOULD LOVE TO HAVE YOUR PROBLEMS

When you, like Lucifer, bear down from the west,
a comet hightailing for intergalactic destruction,
remember the promise of everlasting boredom,

your bones ground down to a fine, useless meal
that even the death birds won't touch with their ten-
foot beaks, so toxic is your halcyon odor.

Think of those poor souls who'd gladly give
their rotting right arm for your general malaise,
your false sense of diurnal entitlement, as you

sweep porches and write your neatly lined poems,
most already two beats in the grave. Time
to worry more, for sooner or later you'll pine

for the days of those panic-struck flights,
the nights that sent your bald heart fluttering
with the fear of wasting another year of your life.

POSTMORTEM

In 1793, during the French Revolution,
      Charlotte Corday was executed
by guillotine for the assassination
      of Jean-Paul Marat. After her head

fell into the basket with a sickening
      thump, like an overripe cantaloupe
or a coconut, the device's carpenter
      picked it up by the hair and slapped it.

According to witnesses, an expression
      of "unequivocal indignation" crossed
her face. As if being beheaded weren't
      enough. What if, at the moment

the living betray me, smacking me
      with the reality that death is the final
indignity, the sound of my own name
      being pronounced gone, the sheet

rises to my eyes, while I still see?

SELF-ELEGY WITH HAND GRENADE

Like a pearl, or an egg,
it waits, my death,

like something that could fit
in your palm.

Bleak, bleak, you say.
Yes, but isn't the way

we always keep
dying beautiful?

If beauty is nothing
but the beginning of terror,

I want to make a career
out of terrorism.

See me there
on the street corner,

exploding myself
in the sun?

*She was a martyr
for beauty*, they'll say.

SELF-PORTRAIT AS KURT COBAIN'S HUNGRY GHOST (WITH AN APPEARANCE BY THÍCH QUẢNG ĐỨC)

Because she wants to believe that death is like the silence one encounters after writing a poem, a silence replete with stillness and the release that comes after the possession of language, the speaker admits she has a hard time imagining herself as a suicide on the other side of the door, still strumming with desire and the karmic fears that kept him trapped inside the coffin of his body, only now there are no hinges and now it's made of glass. Because no one wants to believe that death is not the end of suffering, a reader would not respond well to a poem in which the speaker adopts the persona of a man who has suffered enough and does not deserve to be made into an entity of fire, a Buddhist monk eternally setting himself ablaze. There are limits to what a poem should do. (According to witnesses, after the body burned, the heart remained intact.)

STARMAN TRACTATE: ASHES TO ASHES

I don't know why people say he "left this earth." I get the whole spaceflight metaphor, and I understand that Bowie was not exactly of this earth, in the sense that he was a supernova and thus subject to a different set of gravitational laws, even in death, but still I keep thinking about his cremation and the bulldozer in the background of the "Ashes to Ashes" video. How the body must have burned with a jewel-like flame. How little of him there must have been left.

TRANSFIGURATION

How on earth to describe it,
that moment when the unearthly
    occurs, when one is suspended
        outside the border of time, outside
        the body and its limitations, free-

    falling above some vast design
one can only view from a distance,
    as when I sat in the fragile dusk,
        contemplating the whereabouts
        of my dead friend and suddenly

    I saw it, casualty of my children's play:
plastic god in the shape of an elephant.
    It didn't take much. I so wanted
        to believe: there he is in the loamy
        newborn breath of spring,

    the one still waiting to be born,
and the one who keeps vigil over
    his waiting. I admit I wanted
        to be that one, so in that instant,
        the toy transfigured.

MY PAST LIFE AS A SUPERNOVA

Turns out Whitman wasn't far off: we can reincarnate as a collapsing massive star, sending shockwaves of solar energy through the interstellar medium, and appear, temporarily, as a brand-new star. In fact, we are made of this very energy, and as a result, our supernova consciousness is too subtle to recognize consciousness as such. Only by hacking the password primeval was I able to unlock this mystery. Don't take my word for it: look at the way we burn so brightly when lit from within by the source of our rage. When I die again, I'll come back a saint.

THE GREAT MYSTERIES

Sometimes, when the wind blows a certain way,
I think I can hear the dead laughing.

All they have to do is open their throats,
and the leaves rattle, as the sky makes
a little pathway for their party.

Other times, it's quiet.
The stars burn, but remain hidden.

They may be waving. Maybe not.

ELEGY WITH SPRAY PAINT CAN

Rilke says that what the dead
want of him is that he allow

them the privilege of being dead,
which is, after all, hard work.

What do you want of me, shade?
I ask in the spirit of equanimity,

though the restless footsteps
in the farthest corners

of my brain suggest
otherwise. Can you hear me?

Can you feel my thoughts
tethering your silence

to the page, each line tracing
the arc of your soul's journey

toward some vision of eternity
I can't see? I can't tell you

what to say. If I open my mouth,
only ash will fly out.

But while I have your attention,
let me point out that Rilke

was also right about the living
needing the great mysteries,

even as the dead no longer
need us. Each day, I wait for you

to speak. The first evening,
I watched the sun burn

a hole through the window
of an abandoned apartment

building and took that
as the sign I needed: your name,

star-shaped, gold-flecked,
in relief against the wordless

world you've been given.

GOYA'S *RED BOY*

Perhaps the delicate golden string
he holds like a kite's twine in his bare hands
represents the years allotted to him,

and the magpie at the end of it with the artist's
calling card in its scythed beak is the painter
himself, like the child, Destiny's plaything,

and the caged finches at his satined feet
are the disappearing world of his childhood,
as the diabolical cats crouch menacingly

in the shadows, all eyes and feline hunger,
waiting for the moment when the boy's
attention falters, when the painter drops

his brush because he cannot look
any longer, even as he holds us there, fixed
to the grave of the boy's bright gaze.

NINTH YEAR: WILLOW

Honestly, I'm not sure how I feel about
this year's traditional anniversary gift
(or the traditional anniversary poem,
for that matter), first, because I somewhat
resent the loaded symbolism of the willow,
tree that weeps at the edge of water, mythic
tree of origins that bends and bends but will
not break, and second, because we know
how the last commemorative bonsai
ended up. Rather, I propose we celebrate
the ninth year in peace, no heavy limbs
to weigh us down like Desdemona
as she drowns in a bed of her own unmaking.
Instead, let's do it our way—defy gravity,
                    grow *upward*.

HYSTERECTOMY

It's like I keep forgetting
my purse somewhere,

and then I remember
I have no purse, no phone

buzzing away inside it,
and no one around

to take the call. It was
the wrong number

anyway. It was God
calling. It was a prank

call. But sometimes when
I'm very quiet inside

myself, it sounds like
a widow sobbing.

LIKE RUNNING INTO HILLARY CLINTON IN THE WOODS

Some poems just won't let you go, the way
grief finds you where you least expect it—
in freeway gridlock, for example, or while
watching your kids spin on the Tilt-A-Whirl,
the golden thread of their laughter woven
into sunlight. Some poems, like grief, like anger,
seethe just under the surface of your being,
a Bengal tiger pacing in its cage, its strides
a portent, an omen. Nothing, you believe,
happens for a reason, there is no grand
design or fate, and if that poem really wants
to be written, it will pop out from behind
a tall shrub or tree and shake you just a little,
the way some dreams shake us from sleep.

RECURRING DREAM: ELEVATOR (CO-STARRING PRINCE AND WITH AN UNSCRIPTED APPEARANCE BY EMILY DICKINSON)

Till elevators drop us from our day…
— Hart Crane

Only it's not an elevator, it's a death chamber
    in your parents' backyard, a queue of people

waiting to enter. Prince is ahead of you.
    This is where the dream turns creepy:

you conflate the androgynous figure
    standing next to you in line with the late

rock star because of his real-life death
    in an elevator some weeks later, and now

you're uncertain whether it was really Prince
    you dreamed of, or if you made that up.

You know it's against the rules—one soul
    at a time—but still you can't resist the urge

to calm him when he loses it and then to step
    with him inside. Here's where the dream

turns self-referential: you take his hand—
    your own—and together you fall

through the levels of consciousness, just like
    in that Dickinson poem, only here there is no

snap of the plank, no end of knowing,
      no *then* –. Dearly beloved, let this be

a lesson to you: never try to decode a dream
      through the lens of a poem, especially

a poem by Dickinson. As a matter of fact,
      ban all Dickinsonian dream symbols

from your vocabulary. There are better poets
      to draw on for these sorts of things—Berryman,

for example, Franz Wright, most definitely—
      and besides, as is well known, elevators

do not commonly appear in American poetry
      until the early part of the twentieth century.

GLADIATOR

Today, I think I'll be a gladiator.
I don't know how many poems about gladiators there are,
but I suspect there aren't very many.

I think I'll be that moment after the fatal backstab,
after Maximus finally has his revenge,
driving his blade into the neck of the gurgling Commodus

with a look almost tender in its fury,
the moment before he falls,
when he sees the door and pushes it open,

his family waiting for him on the other side,
his farm restored, the rich fields of silken wheat
all golden in the light of the afterworld.

When you're dead, everything is beautiful.

SELF-PORTRAIT AS KURT COBAIN'S LEFT-HANDED GUITAR

The greatest risk of such a poem is sentimentality. How to render the longing of the object in a way that is both human and inhuman, inevitable and surprising, without lapsing into the obvious clichés? How to portray the subject—in this case, the speaker herself— through the prism of a persona who speaks only through the hands that animate it? The instrument could be anything—a guitar, a scalpel, a blade of grass. What matters is hitting all the right notes at precisely the moment they start to implode, like a stained glass window or a collapsing star. Remember Orpheus, downriver, still shredding his lyre? What matters is the playing.

CACHE LA POUDRE

Tonight the cicadas are deafening.
Nothing to do but lean into despair
the way one leans into a mirror.

All summer you've been dying
in the shopping cart of my mind.
I fill it up with bottles of vinegar.

The river is lonely. It has no home.
Soon your voice will be everywhere.

A YEAR LATER

When I first heard the voice,
I mistook it for something
I had once buried, as if the clouds

had passed across the sun,
and I was exposed, burning.
For months, it went on like that.

I could reach my hand
not under but *through* the veil,
the outlines of the other world

taking shape before me.
Then one day it stopped.
The world was as it had always been,

except that you were gone.

NOTES

"Self-Portrait as Kurt Cobain's Childhood Wound": The parenthetical sentence is from *King Lear* (4.1.53-54).

"My Past Life as a Puritan": The demonic possession of Elizabeth Knapp is one of 14 cases of "witchcraft" Cotton Mather describes in *The Wonders of the Invisible World*, his defense of the Salem Witch Trials.

"Poem in the Manner of the Year in Which I Was Born" owes a debt to David Lehman.

"Self-Portrait as Kurt Cobain's Imaginary Friend": The italicized sentence and "experienced simpleton, emasculated, infantile complainee" are from Kurt Cobain's suicide note.

"Self-Elegy with Hand Grenade": "Like a pearl, or an egg, / it waits" are the last lines of Cody Todd's "In the Suburbia North of Here"; the lines "beauty is nothing / but the beginning of terror" are from "The First Elegy" of Rilke's *Duino Elegies*.

"Self-Portrait as Kurt Cobain's Hungry Ghost": Thích Quảng Đức was the Vietnamese Buddhist monk who self-immolated on a street in Saigon in 1963 in protest of the South Vietnamese government's persecution of Buddhists.

ACKNOWLEDGMENTS

Many thanks to the editors of the following publications in which these poems first appeared, some under different titles:

32 Poems: "Faith"

The Adirondack Review: "Elegy with a Cameo by Linda Ronstadt," "Song While the Children Are Napping," "Your Life Is Meaningless"

Barrow Street: "Fifth Year: Wood"

Beloit Poetry Journal: "The Martian"

B O D Y: "Cache la Poudre," "My Past Life as a Songbird"

The Carolina Quarterly: "The Cemetery Is Full of People Who Would Love to Have Your Problems," "Self-Elegy with Hand Grenade"

Cider Press Review: "My Past Life as a Puritan"

Cimarron Review: "Recurring Dream: Elevator"

Come as You Are: An Anthology of 90s Pop Culture: "Self-Portrait as Kurt Cobain's Imaginary Friend"

DMQ Review: "My Past Life as a Supernova"

Ekphrasis: "Goya's *Red Boy*," "The Young Virgin"

The Ekphrastic Review: "Last Tango in Paris," "Minority Report"

Gargoyle Magazine: "Black Friday"

Green Mountains Review: "Palomas, Ciudad de México"

Harpur Palate: "Ninth Year: Willow," "Transfiguration"

Jam Tarts: "Self-Portrait as Kurt Cobain Wrestling with the Angel," "Self-Portrait as Kurt Cobain's Hungry Ghost," "Self-Portrait as Kurt Cobain's Left-Handed Guitar," "Self-Portrait as Kurt Cobain's Muse"

Kenyon Review: "Lament in the Style of Monica Lewinsky's Blue Dress," "Self-Portrait as Cindy Sherman's Instagram Account"

Literal Latté: "Self-Portrait as Kurt Cobain in Drag," "Self-Portrait as Kurt Cobain's Childhood Wound"

Literary Mama: "Capital I"

LUMINA: "Elegy with Spray Paint Can"

The Massachusetts Review: "Sixth Year: Iron"

New Orleans Review: "Requiem with an Amulet in Its Beak"

Nightjar Review: "A Year Later"

North American Review: "Hysterectomy," "Koko the Gorilla Is Dead," "Like Running into Hillary Clinton in the Woods," "Threnody with a White Ford Bronco Inside It"

Poetry Northwest: "Poem in the Manner of the Year in Which I Was Born"

Quarterly West: "My Brain Is Mad for Baudrillard"

Rattle: Poets Respond: "The Year of the Eclipse"

Rise Up Review: "Fourth of July"

River Styx: "The Great Mysteries"

Salamander: "Meditation," "Postmortem"

Sonora Review: "Starman Tractate: Chameleon, Comedian, Corinthian, and Caricature"

Southern Poetry Review: "Eighth Year: Bronze"

Split Lip Magazine: "My Past Life as a Dinosaur"

Spoon River Poetry Review: "Self-Portrait as the Love Child of Kurt Cobain and Emily Dickinson"

Sugar House Review: "Hunter's Moon, Gettysburg"

Valparaiso Poetry Review: "After the Flood"

What Rough Beast: "Is That a Gun in Your Pocket"

A group of these poems won the 2018 Robert H. Winner Memorial Award from the Poetry Society of America, judged by Airea D. Matthews. "Fourth of July" also appears on the PSA website.

"My Brain Is Mad for Baudrillard," "Poem in the Manner of the Year in Which I Was Born," "Requiem with an Amulet in Its Beak," and "Self-Portrait as Cindy Sherman's Instagram Account" also appear on the Academy of American Poets website.

"Self-Portrait as Kurt Cobain's Muse" will also appear in *More Truly and More Strange: 100 Contemporary American Self-Portrait Poems* (Persea Books, forthcoming 2020).

My sincerest thanks to the members of the Washington Writers' Publishing House for selecting this collection for the Jean Feldman Poetry Prize, with special thanks to Jona Colson and Kathleen Wheaton for their editorial guidance and support. Thanks to my friends and fellow poets Aaron Angello, James Allen Hall, Mark Irwin, Arnold Johnston, Kirun Kapur, Richard Katrovas, Liz Marlow, Airea D. Matthews, and Maggie Smith for reading and commenting on various drafts of this manuscript. I am also grateful to the Maryland State Arts Foundation and the Hood College Board of Associates for awards and grants that supported the writing of this book. Love and gratitude to my family, with profoundest thanks to Robert Eversz, my first and last reader, my alpha and omega everything.

CPSIA information can be obtained
at www.ICGtesting.com
Printed in the USA
LVHW031128161019
634268LV00005B/855/P

9 781941 551202